The Solar Plexus or Abdominal Brain

The Solar Plexus or Abdominal Brain

THERON Q. DUMONT

COSIMOCLASSICS

NEW YORK

There are greater wonders and mysteries wrapped
up in the domain of Nature than have ever been
dreamed of by man in his search for the supernatural.

——from Lesson 1, "The Science of Mental Healing"

Table of Contents

¶

The Four Brains of Man

Man has four brains, and not merely one as is commonly believed to be the case. Man's four brains, each having its separate characteristics and distinctive offices and functions, are as follows: (1) the Cerebrum; (2) the Cerebellum; (3) the Medulla Oblongata; and (4) the Solar Plexus, or Abdominal Brain. The structure, and the respective offices and functions of each of these four brains of Man, are as follows:

(1) **The Cerebrum.** The Cerebrum is the higher and front portion of "the brains" located in the cranium or skull. It consists of two symmetrical halves, which are connected by a broad band of white substance. Each hemisphere is composed of a centre of white substance. surrounded by a gray border, following the convolutions which constitute its external form. The offices and functions of the Cerebrum are as follows: (1) the anterior portions of the cerebral hemispheres are the chief centres of voluntary motion, and of the

active outward manifestations of Intelligence: (2) the individual convolutions constitute separate and distinct centres; and in certain groups of convolutions are localized the centres for various physical movements, i.e., the motions of the eyelids, face, mouth, tongue, ear, neck, hand, foot, etc.

The Cerebellum. The Cerebellum is the hinder and lower part of "the brains" located in the cranium of skull; it is situated beneath the posterior lobes of the Cerebrum, and is about one-seventh the size of the latter. It is composed of white matter in the interior, and of gray matter on the surface. It is divided into two hemispheres, separated on the upper surface by an anatomical process, and on the lower surface by a deep fissure corresponding in form to the Medulla Oblongata. The white centre of the Cerebellum takes on the form of a miniature tree, with trunk, branches, twigs, and leaves—this is known as the "arbor vitæ." The offices and functions of the Cerebellum are as follows: (1) it is concerned with the powers of motion in various ways and forms, in various degrees; and (2) it is held by some authorities to perform certain important offices in connection with the physical phase of the sexual functions and organism.

The Medulla Oblongata. The Medulla Oblongata is the upper and enlarged end of the spinal cord—the extension and prolongation of the latter into the cranium or skull. Its substance resembles that of the spinal cord in its structure of gray and white matter; but it possesses a peculiar and different arrangement of the strands of the cord before it enters into and forms a connection with the brain. In the substance of the Medulla Oblongata are situated the great ganglionic centres which control respiration. deglutition, vomiting, etc. Pressure of the Medulla Oblongata, and not simple strangulation, is held to be the actual cause of death in the process of judicial hanging. From the interior portion of the Medulla Oblongata, and the under surface of the Cerebrum, arise the Cranial Nerves, which emerge from the craninal cavity through openings in the base of the skull; these are distributed to various parts of the head and neck; to the organs of special sense; and to some of the thoracic and abdominal organs. In the posterior and lowermost portion of the substance of the Medulla Oblongata, are located the original sources of certain nerves which indirectly control the organs and functions of respiration.

The Solar Plexus, or Abdominal Brain. The

Solar Plexus, or Abdominal Brain, the functions and offices, the powers and activities, of
which constitute the chief subject matter of
this book, is, as the name indicated, situated
in the abdomen. Some of its filaments, however, accompany the branches of the aorta
(the great artery) which are distributed to
the stomach, intestines, spleen, pancreas, liver,
and certain other organs, but not to the lungs.
It is situated in the upper part of the abdomen,
behind the stomach, in front of the aorta or
great artery, and in front of the pillars of the
diaphragm. Its place is popularly known as
"the pit of the stomach," or back of the point
where the ribs begin to separate and spread
to each side.

The Solar Plexus is the great plexus, i.e.,
network of nerve-fibres, mass of nerve-sub-
stance, etc., of the great Sympathetic Nervous
System. It is composed of both gray and
white nervous substance, or brain-matter,
similar to that of the other three brains of
Man. It receives and distributes nerve-
impulses and currents to all of the abdominal
organs, and supplies the main organs of nutrition, assimilation, etc., with their nervous
energy. It performs most important offices
in the so-called "vegetative life" of the body,
supplying the nerve-energy which is required

for the processes of nutrition, assimilation growth, etc. In fact, it is the great power-house of physical life-energy. The bodily functions cannot be performed without it; when it is injured the entire physical well-being is at once seriously affected; and when it receives a severe shock, death often ensues, a fact which the history of prize-fighting amply illustrates.

Its name, "solar," was bestowed upon it by reason of (1) its central position; (2) the fact that its filaments extend in all directions to the important abdominal organs, like the rays of the sun; and (3) the fact that it is recognized as being the power-house, and great reservoir of "life force," just as the sun is the great power-house and reservoir of material energy of our solar system.

The Sympathetic Nervous System, over which it presides, is that great division of the nervous system which regulates and energizes the important functions of the organs upon which physical life depends, and by which it is sustained. Bichet terms this division of the nervous system, "the nervous system of organic life," because, as he pointed out, "it seems to regulate—almost or quite independently of the will—the due performance of the functions of the organs of respiration, circulation, and digestion."

Bailey says: "Functionally, the Sympathetic System is quite distinct from the Cerebro-Spinal System. It has been called the system of vegetative existence, because of its presiding over the processes of nutrition and growth, the so-called 'vegetative functions,' in contra-distinction to the Cerebro-Spinal System, which presides over such distinctly animal faculties as sensation, motion, and intellect. The Sympathetic System controls the so-called automatic mechanisms of the body, the rhythmical beating of the heart, contraction and dilation of the arteries, the peristaltic action of the gastro-intenstinal tract, the contraction of smooth muscle wherever found, and the control of the secretions of various glands, etc." So, it may be seen, the Solar Plexus presides over a very important region of physical life.

The Solar Plexus both receives and transmits nerve impulses, just as do the better-known brains of Man. Its distributed filaments contain both afferent (inward conduction) and efferent (outward conducting) nerve-fibres, just as is the case with the other three brains. Its ganglia (series of knotted nervous substance) are true nerve-centers, and from them emerge and pass the filaments of nerve-force distribution to the involuntary muscles of the organs under its control, and to the secreting-cells of the various glands, etc., which depend upon it for their nerve supply. Dr. Byron Robinson, who first applied the term "The Abdominal Brain" to the Solar Plexus, says of it that: "By the use of this term, I mean to convey the idea that it is endowed with the high powers and phenomena of a great nervous centre; that it can organize, multiply, and diminish forces."

It is easily seen why an injury to the Solar Plexus seriously disturbs the life-processes, and why a severe blow so paralyzes the vital organs that death ensues almost immediately. A man may survive a serious injury to any one of his other three brains; but a serious injury to the Solar Plexus, or Abdominal Brain, strikes right to his seat of life—and that life ceases to manifest itself further. If Man may properly say of any portion of his physical being, "Here is the seat of my life; here is where I live!" the Solar Plexus, or Abdominal Brain, surely is that particular part or portion of his physical being.

As an additional illustration of the essential part played by the Solar Plexus, or Abdominal Brain, in the processes of physical life, we have the well-known fact that it is found fully formed and perfect, and even then performing some important functioning, in the human embryo or foetus at a very early stage—at a stage in which the "skull brain" of the developing unborn creature is a merely pulpy mass of substance, incapable of performing any function whatsoever. Moreover, in those cases of the birth of abnormal infants—babies born without a "skull brain" or perfected spinal cord—the Solar Plexus, or Abdominal Brain, has been found to be perfectly developed, and to perform its full functions; and under such circumstances the child has lived for months before delivery, and in some cases for some time afterward.

So much for the offices and functions which orthodox physiologists freely ascribe to the Solar Plexus, or Abdominal Brain. Other careful investigators take up the inquiry at this point, but carry the story much further. Not alone modern scientific investigators; but also many very ancient investigators, such as the oriental occultists and sages, who many centuries ago recognized certain subtle functions and offices of this wonderful "fourth brain" of Man, and taught their students many valuable methods of effectively employing its finer forces and hiddent energies. In this book, we shall try to convey to you the essence and fundamental substance of these higher teachings concerning the Solar Plexus, or Abdominal Brain—the Fourth Brain of Man!

II

The Emotional Centre

One of the great facts concerning the Solar Plexus, or Abdominal Brain, which fact is not as yet generally recognized by modern psychology and physiology, but which has been known for centuries by the occultists, and which is now becoming recognized by the advanced minds of modern science, is this important fact, i.e., that **the Solar Plexus is the seat of the emotional nature of Man.** In short, that the part popularly held to be played by "the heart," is in reality performed by the Solar Plexus, or Abdominal Brain, the great centre of the Sympathetic Nervous System.

That there is an important relation between the emotional states and the physical organism, everyone knows. We know that fear, dread, and suspense are accompanied by a sinking or even a "sick" feeling at the pit of the stomach. We know that the heart beats rapidly when we are excited, angry, or in love. We know, particularly of later years, that emotional states react upon the physical organs, working physiological changes in them, and often exercising a decided influence upon the health or lack of health in the organs affected. You have had presented to your attention hundreds of books reaching "the effect of mind upon body."

Likewise, we know that the condition of certain of the physical organs has much to do with our "state of feeling." We know from experience the state of "blues" and emotional depression caused by the failure of the liver to function properly. We know also the lack of energy, and the feeling of heaviness caused by the constipated condition of the bowels. We know the generally "crabbed" feelings caused by indigestion and dyspepsia. We know the heavy, sluggish feelings caused by breathing the heavy air of an illy ventilated room. We know the nervous, excitable, hysterical emotional states arising from abnormal conditions of the sexual organism.

Dr. H. A. Parkyn calls our attention to similar effect of body upon mind, in the following words: "The moment a man's circulation begins to run down, owing to stinted nutrition, we find that the first symptoms appear in the head. The brain failing to receive its accustomed amount of blood, such troubles as impaired memory, inability to concentrate the

attention, sleeplessness, nervousness, irritabil-
ity, the blues and slight headaches develop.
. . . When the blood supply is not up to the
normal standard, the mental functions are
interfered with to a degree corresponding to
the reduction of the circulation. The reasoning power becomes weakened, and the stead-
iest mind commences to vaccilate. Fears and
hallucinations of every description may fill the
mind, and every impression received is likely
to be greatly distorted or misconstrued. Mel-
ancholia with a fear of impending danger is
often present."

Another point brought out in the investiga-
tions and experiments of modern psychology
is that **"no emotion is completely experienced
until its physical states are expressed."** A
leading psychologist illustrates this fact as
follows: "The emotion of anger begins to
arise; but it will not be complete until it has
found expression in some of the bodily organs.
There is a scowl upon the brow, a compression
of the lips, a muscular tension of the hands, a
quickened heart-beat. **If these bodily changes
arose without an idea, their effects would be
transmitted to the mind, and we should have
feeling as the result.** Now the results of this
physical activity, muscular tension and expression, are reflected back upon a mind in

which the emotion of anger is developing. The feeling from this reflected wave is the factor necessary to complete the emotion. So important is this wave of expressive physical expression dashing back upon the mental state that some have even concluded that an emotion does not really **begin** until the sensations from the physical expression of the idea are reflected back on consciousness."

Professor William James emphasized this fact very strongly. He says: "My theory is that the bodily changes follow directly the perception of the exciting fact, and that our feeling of these changes as they occur is the emotion. Particular perceptions certainly do produce widespread bodily effects by a sort of immediate physical influence, antecedent to the arousal of an emotion or emotional idea. Every one of the bodily changes, whatsoever it may be, is felt, acutely or obscurely, the moment it occurs. If we fancy some strong emotion, and then try to abstract from our consciousness of it all the feelings of its bodily symptoms, we have nothing left behind. Disembodied human emotion is a sheer nonentity. For us, emotion dissociated from all bodily feelings is inconceivable. The more closely I scrutinize my emotional states, the more certain I become that whatever 'coarse' affections

and passions I have are in very truth consti-
tuted by, and made up of, those physical
changes we ordinarily call our expression or
consequence."

Professor James, at other times, made the
following statements supporting this position:
"We feel sorry because we cry, angry because
we strike, afraid because we tremble, and not
that we cry strike, or tremble **because** we are
sorry, angry, or fearful." "Objects do excite
bodily changes by a preorganized mechanism.
These changes are so indefinitely numerous
and subtle that the entire organism may be
called a sounding board for changes in emotional consciousness. Every one of these
changes is **felt** acutely or obscurely, the moment it occurs." James explained that by
"exciting object" he meant "the entire situation; the object as accompanied by its associated train of ideas and tinged with agree-
ableness or disagreeableness." The theory,
thus modified and explained, has been stated
by others as follows: "The theory merely as-
serts that 'the rank feeling of excitement,'
characteristic of emotion is mediated by the
organic suggestions aroused by our instinctive
physical reaction upon the situation."

The supporters of this theory appeal to the
following general facts to support it: "(1) In

pathological cases, where there is complete organic anæsthesia, there is also an entire absence of emotion; (2) Emotions may be set up by purely physiological means, i.e., by the action of drugs and stimulants, in which ideas and judgments play no part at all. Palpitation of the heart and feelings of suffocation produce fear; a certain amount of alcohol produces exhilaration and cheerfulness; (3) Conditions of the glands result in specific emotional disturbances."

The more conservative authorities, while admitting the value of the "James-Lange Theory" (just stated in general outline), are inclined to the opinion that it over-emphasizes an important element of emotional feeling and phenomena, while under-emphasizing the other equally important element, i.e., the ideaitive element. As an authority has said: "Those who cannot accept the theory as an adequate account of the emotive process, nevertheless grant that its formulation has been, and may yet be, useful in various ways. It lays emphasis upon certain components of emotion that are too often overlooked, and so increases the accuracy of our descriptions. It warns us against an over estimation of idea as compared with bare sentiency; and it suggests a method of settling, or at least helping

to settle, the old and vexed question of the
classification of the emotions."

We are not here concerned with the accept-
ance of the James-Lange theory in its en-
tirety. The above statement of the conservative psychologists is sufficient for our purpose.
The recognition of the important part played
by the physical organs in the processes of
emotional feeling and expression, is sufficient
for us here.

We may mention, in passing, however, that
one should not overlook the fact that the
lower animals in whom the reasoning and in-
tellectual faculties are comparatively quite
undeveloped, nevertheless experience and ex-
press even stronger and more violent feelings
than does Man, in whom the conscious "idea"
is far more in evidence. Moreover, even in the
human race, strong feelings and emotions are
experienced and manifested by even those of
comparatively undeveloped ideative powers.

Feeling, in short, is far more basic that is
ideative thought—far more primitive and
fundamental in nature—and is evidently
seated in far more primitive and fundamental
nervous centres than the "thinking brain." It
evidently belongs to "brains" and great nervous centres which were produced in the evo-

lution of life long before the developed "thinking brains."

Moreover, the close relationship of emotional feeling and the great physical organs regulated and supplied with energy by the Sympathetic Nervous System, and not by the Cerebro-Spinal System, clearly indicates that the "seat of the emotions" must be looked for in the great "brain," or nervous energy-centre of the Sympathetic Nervous System. That "brain," or great nervous centre, as you have seen, is none other than the Solar Plexus, or Abdominal Brain,—the centre of life and life action, and of the elementary and fundamental activities and processes of life.

Thus, you see, the advanced thought of modern science is fast approaching the position of the ancient occultists, and is adding modern testimony to the teachings of these great ancient teachers—the position and teaching that the Solar Plexus, or Abdominal Brain, is the great centre and seat of the feelings and emotions; the source and origin from which all of our strong and elemental feelings and emotions arise and from which they flow. This being seen, it is also perceived that if we wish to regulate, control and direct our emotional nature, we must begin at that seat and centre thereof—the Solar Plexus. In the next chapter, we shall give you the teachings concerning this regulation, control and direction of the feelings and emotions, through the awakening and use of the Solar Plexus itself.

III
Emotional Control

In the preceding chapter, we made clear to you the fact that the emotional feelings of Man have their seat and centre in the Solar Plexus, or Abdominal Brain—that great centre and power-house of the Sympathetic Nervous System which operates the great internal physical organs. We have also indicated to you that in order to regulate, control and direct your emotional nature, you must begin by regulating the activity of the Solar Plexus.

The reason of this last fact is simple. It being seen that (1) there is no complete emotional state without the physical organism being involved; and (2) that the physical organism is under the direct control of the Sympathetic Nervous System; and (3) that the central-station and power-house of the Sympathetic Nervous System is the Solar Plexus, or Abdominal Brain; then it logically follows that (4) if there is possible any control, regulation and direction of the emotional nature, it must be found in the control, regulation and direction of the Solar Plexus. The premises of this argument being admitted, as they must be according to the facts of the case, the conclusion logically follows, and must also be admitted.

That the emotional nature may be regulated, controlled and directed is a fact known to all persons who have escaped the bondage of elemental and instinctive feeling, and who have learned that it is possible to exercise control over their passions, emotions and feelings. Such control, in fact, is necessary in our civilized and social life. The strong men of the race have exercised it to a great extent; lack of such control is generally held to be a mark of weak character and of flabby will. It is only the lower animal, or uncultured and semi-barbarous man who exercises no control of his feelings and passions, his emotional impulses and actions.

But in most cases this control has been effected by a sheer effort of will—this effort tending to hold back, restrain or control the action naturally tending to follow the rise of the emotional feeling. Very few persons realize that there is possible a far more direct method of controlling and directing the emotional feelings.

Those who have learned the possibility of the direct control of the emotional feelings in the way above mentioned, are usually found to follow one or both of the two following general methods, viz.: (1) the method of "holding the thought" of the opposite emotional feeling, thus neutralizing the feeling sought to be eliminated or controlled; or (2) the method of deliberately assuming the physical emotions associated with the feelings directly opposed to the ones sought to be suppressed. By reversing these methods, desirable emotional feelings may be cultivated, encouraged, stimulated, and developed, i.e., by "holding the thought" of them, and by deliberately assuming their associated physical actions.

These two above stated methods are quite scientific, and have been employed by many with excellent results—many have "made over" their emotional natures and characters in just this way. We advise you to hold fast to these methods, and to adapt them to the additional method which we shall present to you in a moment. This new method, in fact, has the same underlying principle—but it enters into the centre or "kernel" of that principle, while the others merely touch its surface. In this new method, you get right to

the centre of the emotional activities—to the
Solar Plexus itself—instead of merely dealing
with the incidental activities related to that
centre.

Here is the mechanism employed in this
new system of the control of the emotional
feelings by awakening and controlling the
Solar Plexus. In the first place, the Cerebro-
Spinal Nervous System, controlled by the
Cerebrum—the seat of thoughts and ideas—is
directly connected with the Sympathetic Nervous System, controlled by the Solar Plexus,
or Abdominal Brain,—the seat of feelings and
vital processes; they are connected by means
of many delicate nervous filaments, or "con-
nective nerves." These "connecting nerves"
are both efferant and afferent—both sending
and receiving. They are like telegraph wires,
or telephone wires, connecting the two great
systems and their respective centres. Over
them pass the messages which, on the one
hand, cause the physical states to arouse
mental states; and, on the other hand, the
messages causing the mental states, or ideas,
to arouse physical states.

In this way, and by means of this inter-
communication between the two system and
their respective "brains," we have (1) on the
one hand the phenomenon of the disturbed

liver, stomach, bowels, spleen, glands, sexual organism, etc., arousing corresponding "ideas" in the mind—which we know to be of common occurrence; and, on the other hand, we have (2) the phenomenon of "ideas" held in the mind arousing the activity of the physical organs, such as the stomach, bowels, liver, spleen, heart, sexual organism, etc.,—which we also know to be of common occurrence, and which gives us the key to the "mind over body" methods, "mental healing," "suggestion," etc. If there were no such connecting links, or nerves, between the two systems and their respective "brains," none of the above phenomena would be manifested, and Body and Mind would act independently of each other—though in such case there would be a speedy dissolution of living partnership, and death would come in due course.

In ordinary cases, this interchange of messages and orders, from one system to the other, is performed unconsciously and instinctively by the nervous mechanism of the individual—he is neither aware of the process, nor does he consciously will its performance. But the ancient occultists discovered, many centuries ago, that the individual could consciously and deliberately send messages from the Cerebrum, or "thinking brain," to the

Solar Plexus, or "feeling and vital-process brain." And advanced modern psychologists are now making the same discovery, though they give to the old occultists no credit, but bestow new names upon the process—the facts remain the same, however.

The Cerebrum, or "thinking brain," while largely influenced by the Solar Plexus, or "feeling brain"—far more influenced by it than most persons realize, in fact—nevertheless can and does exert a tremendous influence over the latter, even without the conscious use of the will and attention. When the individual, however, deliberately turns his conscious attention to the matter, and uses his will in connection with the process, then the Cerebrum, or "thinking brain" exerts a tremendously increased power and influence over the Solar Plexus, or "feeling brain." It is able to dominate the latter to a great extent, and the latter may be easily trained to accept its "suggestions," its demands, and its commands.

In order to exercise this control of the Cerebrum over the Solar Plexus, it is first necessary to arouse the dormant consciousness of the Solar Plexus. The Solar Plexus ordinarily exists in an almost "sleeping" state; or, more correctly, in a state similar to that of

the person "walking or talking in his sleep."
Only in case of great danger to the individual
—in cases of great need to the whole organism—in cases of threatened danger to both
nervous systems and both "brains"—does the
Solar Plexus "wake up" for the time being and
"get busy" in overcoming the obstacles and
averting the danger. The important fact,
however, is this: that the Solar Plexus **can** be
awakened under certain circumstances.

This being perceived by the ancient occultists, they began to devise means whereby they
might awaken the Solar Plexus, at will, under
certain circumstances. These methods they
finally discovered, and adopted; which discovery gave them the key to the practical methods of influencing, directing and controlling
the activities of the Sympathetic Nervous
System, ad also certain other activities with
which we shall become acquainted as we
proceed.

In Chapters V and VI, of this book, we shall
give you the details of the methods of Awakening the Solar Plexus, and of influencing and
directing its activities in general. We defer
this explanation and instruction for the present, because the same is as much related to
certain other features of our instruction as
to that of Emotional Control. The statements

which we shall now make concerning Emotional Control must be read in the light of the special instructions contained in chapters to which we have just alluded; and the directions given below must be employed in connection with the general directions given regarding the processes of "Awakening the Solar Plexus" and "Using the Solar Plexus," as given in the said chapters.

Having awakened the Solar Plexus, and having learned how to give to it the desired suggestions, demands and commands, the matter of causing it to control, direct and arouse the emotional feelings becomes quite simple. Here is the instruction in a nutshell:

Having awakened the Solar Plexus, and having learned the art of suggesting ideas to it, proceed as follows: Tell the Solar Plexus, or "feeling brain," just what you wish it to do for you in the matter of arousing or repressing emotional feelings. Tell it what emotoinal feelings you wish it to develop and encourage, and which you wish it to restrain or repress. Say to it, at the appropriate times: "I wish to feel Happy, or Cheerful; I wish to feel Courageous and Confident, etc.," as the case may be. Or, on the other hand, tell it: "I wish you to prevent the feeling of Fear, or of Depression, or of Excitement, or of Anger,

etc." as the case may be. You will find it a willing helper, and a helpful friend, once you have awakened it properly, and satisfied it of your real relationship to it.

IV

Vitality and Health

That the Solar Plexus, or Abdominal Brain, should be able to exercise an important influence and power over the Health and Vitality of the individual is perceived immediately when we realize its relation to the organs performing the important functions of life. The Solar Plexus, as you have seen, is the great central storehouse of nervous energy, or "life force," of the physical body. It sends to this organ, and to that gland, the supply of nervous energy and vital force which is necessary to animate and energize those parts of the body, and the other parts adjacent thereto.

To understand the importance of this nervous energy or vital force which is controlled and dispensed by the Solar Plexus, it is necessary only to consider the activities performed by means of its power. For instance, we find that the processes of digestion, assimilation, nutrition and elimination are possible only when the supply of vital force is sufficient. Likewise, we find that the processes of the circulation of the blood are dependent upon the supply of the vital force.

As a writer has said: "Our food is digested and transformed into the nourishing substances of the blood; then carried through the arteries to all parts of the body, where it is absorbed by the cells and used to replace the worn-out material, the latter then being carried back through the veins to the lungs, where the waste-matter is burned-up, and the balance again sent on its journey through the arteries re-charged with the life-giving oxygen." All of these processes are performed by the power of the life force which is sent to the organs by the Solar Plexus, and which serves to energize and to animate them; and by means of which the organs are enabled to perform their functions.

Moreover, the Solar Plexus not only sends the vital force to these important physical organs, but it also exercises a control over them in a way so closely resembling a mental control that many writers have spoken of the presence of "something like intelligence" being manifested in the performance and direction of the vital processes. This "something like intelligence" has been explained under various theories of "unconscious mind," "sub-

conscious mind," etc.; but whatever these
"minds" may be at the last analysis, it is in-
disputable that they employ the Sympathetic
Nervous System as their mechanism—and
that the Solar Plexus, or Abdominal Brain,
is "the brains" of that system, just as the
Cerebrum is "the brains" of the Cerebro-
Spinal System. So, notwithstanding the
"other mind" theories, we must always come
back to the Solar Plexus, or Abdominal Brain,
when we wish to see how that "other mind"
works.

Dr. Schofield says: "The unconscious mind
has another very important office, i.e., the
nutrition or general maintenance of the
body." Dr. Hudson says: "The subjective
mind has an absolute control of the functions,
conditions and sensations of the body." Von
Hartmann says: "The explanation that unconscious psychical activity itself appro-
priately forms and maintains the body, has
not only nothing to be said against it, but has
all possible analogies from the most different
departments of physical and animal life in its
favor, and appears to be as scientifically certain as is possible in the inference from effect
to cause."

Dr. Schofield presents the following striking
picture of the presence of "unconscious mind"

in the vital processes of the physical body. "It has often been a mystery how the body thrives so well with so little oversight or care on the part of its owner. No machine could be constructed, nor could any combination of solids or liquids in organic compounds, regulate, control, counteract, help, hinder or arrange for the continual succession of differing events, foods, surroundings and conditions which are constantly affecting the body. And yet, in the midst of this ever-changing and varying succession of influences, the body holds on its course of growth, health, nutrition and self-maintenance with the most marvellous constancy.

"We perceive, of course, clearly, that the best of qualities—regulation, control, etc., etc., —are all **mental** qualities, and at the same time we are equally clear that by no self-examination can we say that we **consciously** exercise any of these mental powers over the organic processes of our bodies. One would think, then, that the conclusion is sufficiently simple and obvious—that they must be used **unconsciously**; in other words, it is, and can be nothing else than **unconscious mental powers** that control, guide and govern the functions and organs of the body."

Not only do these "unconscious mental forces" direct the activities of the organs of the physical body, but they also perform important healing work in case of disease and wounds, acting just as would a force that was "something like intelligence." This healing power inherent in the organism has been called "the healing power of nature," the "vis vita," the "vis medicatrix naturæ," or "nature's efforts," etc. Its presence has been recognized by all great physicians and medical teachers. Here are a few testimonies to its presence and power:

Dr. Patton says: "By the term 'efforts of nature' we mean a certain curative or restorative principle, or 'vis vita,' implanted in every living or organized bcly, constantly operative for its repair, preservation and health. This instinctive endeavor to repair the human organism is signally shown in the event of a severed or lost part, as a finger for instance; for nature, unaided, will repair and fashion a stump equal to one from the hands of an eminent surgeon. Nature, unaided, may be equally potent in ordinary illness. Many individuals, even when severely ill, either from motives of economy, prejudice, or skepticism, remain at rest in bed, under favorable hy-

giene, regimen, etc., and speedily get well
without a physician or medicine."

Dr. Schofield says: "The 'vis medicatrix
naturæ' is a very potent factor in the ameliori-
ation of disease, if it only be allowed fair play.
An exercise of faith, as a rule, suspends the
operation of adverse influences, and appeals
strongly to the inner and underlying faculty
of vital force (i.e., the unconscious mind)."
Dr. Bruce says: "We are compelled to ac-
knowledge a power of natural recovery inherent in the body—a similar statement has
been made by writers on the principle of medicine in all ages. The body possesses a means
and mechanism for modifying or neutralizing
influences which it cannot directly overcome.
A natural power of the prevention and repair
of disorders and disease has a real and as
active an existence within us, as have the ordinary functions of the organs themselves."
Hippocrates said: "Nature is the physician of
diseases." Dr. Holmes says: "Whatever other
theories we hold, we must recognize the 'vis
medicatrix naturæ' in some shape or other."

Thus, you see, that great regulative, directive, and therapeutic activities of "Nature,"
which are manifested in the human physical
body, are seen to be mental or quasi-mental in
their essential nature—mind of some degree

is perceived to be at work there. The life-processes are seen to be mind-processes. There is no life-activity without mind activity —the two are inextricably combined and correlated. This fact is thoroughly recognized by the practitioners and students of "mental healing," "suggestive therapy," etc., and their efforts are accordingly directed to "reach the mind" of the individual, in order to "set the mind to work" in the direction of restoration of normal healthy functioning and activity. But **what** "mind" should be reached for this purpose? In **what** brain does that "mind" function and have its seat? Not in the ordinary "thinking mind," to be sure—for the vital processes are not under the control of **that** mind and its brains, though its thoughts and beliefs reflect upon the mind which really is concerned, as we know.

No; the only logical conclusion is that the vital processes and physical organs are under the direction and control of that "mind" which may be called the "instinctive mind" (because it is possessed by the lower animals as well as by man)—which mind has control of the instinctive activities of the physical body, such as we have mentioned. And as every "mind" must have a brain through which to function and manifest itself, we nat-

urally look for the brain or brains of this "instinctive mind." Where? Nowhere else than
in that great centre of physical life and organic control—the Solar Plexus, or Abdominal
Brain. The answer is so obvious that no one
can miss it.

The importance of the above discovery lies
in the fact that just as the "brain-minds" of
all living things can be aroused and appealed
to, so can the "brain-mind" of the Solar
Plexus, or Abdominal Brain, be aroused and
appealed to. if one proceeds properly. The
"brain-mind" of the Solar Plexus, once
aroused, become amenable and subject to appeals, demands, commands, suggestions, etc.,
properly made to it. Here, then, we have a
direct and immediate method of "mental
treatment"—a method which really includes
the active principle of all of the other methods.
A method so simple, so direct, and so effective,
that anyone may apply it, and any organ may
be reached without physical methods. In the
following chapters on "Awakening the Solar
Plexus" and "Using the Solar Plexus," you
will be given further and more detailed par-
ticulars concerning methods of this kind. But,
first of all, you must thoroughly grasp the
fundamental principle involved, i.e., (1) that
the physical organs and activities are con-

trolled by the "instinctive mind"; (2) that the
"instinctive mind" has its seat in the Solar
Plexus, or Abdominal Brain; and (3) that the
"instinctive mind" may be reached and appealed to, when the Solar Plexus—its "brains"
—is aroused and awakened into a state of conscious attention. This is the whole matter in
a nutshell—the rest is merely finding effective
methods of manifesting the principle.

V

Awakening the Solar Plexus

In a preceding chapter of this book, you have seen that the "mind" of the Solar Plexus, or Abdominal Brain—that "instinctive mind" which is to the latter what the "thinking mind" is to the Cerebrum—exists in what may be called a state of semi-sleep, or perhaps more correctly, in a state of semi-consciousness closely resembling that of the sleep-walker who intelligently performs tasks without being fully conscious thereof. In cases of great need, or of threatened danger to the organism, the "instinctive mind" of the Solar Plexus **does** wake up; and in such cases manifests a far greater degree of consciousness than normally expressed by it.

From the above, however, it must not be understood that the "instinctive mind" of the Solar Plexus is ever "asleep" in the sense of not being able to attend to its offices and directive functions. On the contrary, its state of semi-sleep, or semi-consciousness, really arises by reason of its close concentration upon its special tasks just referred to. Its condition of consciousness is very similar to that of the workman, student, or inventor who has so closely concentrated upon the work at hand that he has become practically unconscious of the things of the outside world. You, yourself, have often manifested a similar state when you were reading an interesting book, when you were "buried in your newspaper," or when you were engrossed in the performance of some task to which you have devoted your entire and undivided attention—to which you have given your "whole mind" for the time being.

The "instinctive mind" of the Solar Plexus is not asleep or semi-conscious in the sense of "being asleep at the switch," as the current phrase expresses the idea. On the contrary it is "on the job" to such an extent that it is practically "dead to all the world" other than that "job." It is a most faithful and tireless worker, never sleeping (in the usual sense of the term), and always concerned with the great work under its direction and charge. Were it to "go to sleep," actually—were it to take a rest, or "go on a strike"—the vital processes would cease, and death would speedily result. But, for all that, so far as the outside world is concerned, it may be considered as "asleep," or at least wrapped in revery to such an extent that it must be "awakened" in order to obtain its attention fully.

Passing over the academic terms and technicalities of the psychologists—and also the strange occult terms and theories of the ancient sages who taught along these lines—let us get right down to the practical, everyday description of the methods employed to "Awaken the Solar Plexus." In the first place, you must proceed just as you would in the case of a man who was so wrapped up in his work, so much engrossed with his task, that his whole attention was given there; and who, consequently, was practically unconscious of your presence and your desire to communicate with him. How would you proceed in such a case, and with such a person? Well, in the first place, you would probably endeavor to **attract his attention** by means of tapping his shoulder insistently, until he "woke up"; then, after he had "come out of his trance" (again employing the popular, humorous terminology), you would address him earnestly and forcefully. Well then, this is precisely the method followed in "Awakening the Solar Plexus."

But, you say, we cannot "tap the shoulder" of the Solar Plexus. But, we answer, we can

do this figuratively—we can substitute a physical method which proceeds along the same
lines, and which will produce a similar result.
Here is the method:

(1) Take a few deep, regular breaths; and
then finally, after you have established a regular breathing rhythm, **hold the inhaled
breath instead of exhaling it**—but only for a
few moments, just enough to interrupt the
established rhythm, and,

(2) At the moment when, according to the
established rhythm, the breath should be exhaled, you must, instead (while holding the
breath), employ your abdominal muscles so
that you will (a) **press downward and outward upon the "pit of the stomach"**; and then
(b) **while exhaling the breath, draw in the
same muscles so as to reverse the preceding
motion.** This **outward and inward motion
(accompanied by the breathing) to be performed three times.** Then breathe normally
for a few minutes, resting yourself. The whole
process will have occupied but a few seconds
of time. Then repeat the process, several
times; but use moderation and do not tire
yourself. This process, for certain reasons,
serves to arouse the attention of the "instinctive mind" in the Solar Plexus—just as "the
tap on the shoulder" arouses the man wrapped

in concentrated thought, reverie, or meditation.

(3) While performing the above breathing-method—the "tap on the shoulder"—you must also give the "instinctive mind" the equivalent of the verbal command to "Wake up, old fellow," or "Come out of it!" which would have been used in the case of the meditative friend who was wrapped in thought when you wished to get his attention. This you may do by concentrating your Directive Thought on the "pit of the stomach," and sending the mental message: **"Wake up, Solar Plexus; Give me your attention!"**

You will probably find that you can send a more forceful mental message by actually forming the words with your lips and tongue, just as if you were softly whispering them. In addressing the "instinctive mind," proceed just as you would if the Solar Plexus were a separate and distinct entity—an individual being with mind. The more nearly you can carry out this idea of addressing the Solar Plexus as if it were an individual, the more effective will your demands, commands, and suggestions become. Never mind the technical reason for this fact: don't bother about theories, but stick fast to the actual and practical working out of things.

In the above method you have employed (1) the equivalent for the physical "tap on the shoulder," and (2) the equivalent for the usual "Wake up!" verbal awakener applied to the meditative friend. But, **after this,** what would you do or say to that friend whom you had roused from his concentration or meditation? You would "get down to business," and begin to say what you had to say to him, would you not? Of course, you would. Well then, this is just what you have to do with the "instinctive mind" of the Solar Plexus. And here is how you should proceed to do it.

Having Awakened the Solar Plexus, and having secured the attention of its "instinctive mind," you should proceed to establish harmonious relations with it. You may do this by holding the mental attitude expressed in the following words, and by "sending the thought," you will do well to actually speak the words softly, as above indicated—this plan will greatly aid you in forming the clear thought which you wish to send to the "instinctive mind." And, above all, do not lose sight of the fact that you are to address that "instinctive mind" of the Solar Plexus, just as you would another individual; the more nearly you can do this, the more earnest you can carry out this idea, the better you can carry out this idea, the better you can "throw yourself into the part," the more effective will be your results.

Now then, you are ready to calmly address yourself to the Solar Plexus—that is, to its "instinctive mind." The following illustrative "talk" will give you the general idea of the way to proceed:

"Hello! Solar Plexus! listen to me! This is your friend the Thinking Mind talking to you. We are co-workers, you know. You work down in the engine room, keeping the machinery going, the fires burning, the boilers in good condition—the whole body depends upon you for efficient work in your department. I work up here on the deck; keeping the boat steered properly; keeping a sharp lookout for dangers; keeping you well supplied with proper fuel for your furnaces, sufficient water for your boilers, and sufficient oil for your machinery. Each of us need the other. I need you to keep the machinery going; and you need me to steer the ship and to look out for dangers. Let us work together with a better understanding. I promise to send you nothing but the best fuel, and to refrain from sending down to you anything which may cause trouble with your fires, or clog up your grates. I will pay attention to any messages of disapproval which you may send me; and in short will treat you properly, according to Nature's requirements and laws.

"On the other hand, I want you to pay attention to· my properly-worded requests for improved service by any of the organs which are reporting trouble to me here above deck— I want you to get busy and get such organs in better condition, so that they may render better service. I also want you to help me to restrain and restrict undesirable emotions— you can do this by regulating the physical expression and excitement connected with emotional feeling; and I want you to aid me in having and expressing helpful and beneficial emotional feeling. I also want you to help me in other ways of which I shall tell you later. Now then, Solar Plexus, let us pull together, so as to attain better results for both of us. Let us have confidence in each other—let us trust one another—let us get busy and strive for better results for both of us, and for the entire organism."

In the succeeding chapter, this subject is explained in a little further detail.

VI

Using the Solar Plexus

In the preceding chapter of this book, we left you at the place in which you had established harmonious relations with the "instinctive mind" of your Solar Plexus. Before proceeding further, we wish to impress upon you that this idea of "talking to the Solar Plexus" is not a mere fanciful notion, or mere illustrative presentation. It is a popularly expressed fact, based upon sound scientific psychological method. Its ordinary scientific name is "auto-suggestion"; but it goes far further than ordinary auto-suggestion, for it really establishes an actual connection between two "minds"—between two "brains"—though these two "minds" and two "brains" happen to belong to the same individual. Never mind the technical theories, or academic terms—get busy with the practical methods, so as to get the actual results.

Now then, having become acquainted with your Solar Plexus, and it with you--having established mutual harmony, confidence and co-ordinated effort—you may proceed to give the Solar Plexus more definite and specific directions and suggestions. In doing this, however, always try to keep in mind the idea that you are really talking to another individual entity; and, accordingly, proceed to explain matters, and to point out means and ways of action, just as you would in case of actual conversation with another individual. The following general suggestions and directions should prove interesting and instructive to you.

Emotional Control. The Solar Plexus may be called upon to aid you in either arousing or repressing emotional feelings. By exerting a control upon the physical organs concerned with the expression and manifestation of emotional feeling—by controlling the glands, secretions, reflexes, etc.—it is able either to "shut off" the current of a rising emotional feeling, or else to "turn on" an additional current of a rising emotional feeling. By explaining to the Solar Plexus' "instinctive mind," the reasons why certain emotional states of feeling are desirable or undesirable, advantageous or disadvantageous, it will willingly co-operate with you in repressing and restricting, or else in stimulating and encouraging, any emotional state to which you 'all

its attention. Explain the whole matter to it
—as one good friend or "partner" to another
—and ask it to co-operate with you; it will
gladly do so, once it understands the reason
and just what is required of it.

You will find this co-operation very valuable in cases in which you wish to stimulate
and increase the feeling of Courage, and to
repress and restrain that of Fear. Likewise
when you wish to restrain and restrict the
feeling of Gloom, Depression, and Discourage-
ment, and to increase that of Confidence, Encouragement, and thus acquire the general
"Bright, Cheerful and Happy" feeling. It will
aid you in inhibiting the rise of Anger—a
tremendous achievement, for Anger and Fear
are the two great harmful emotional feelings,
the first destroying by burning-up, and the
second destroying by freezing-up.

Here is the thing in a nut-shell: **Tell the
Solar Plexus the whole story; what you wish
to accomplish with its help; why you wish to
accomplish this; and just what you wish it to
do for you in the matter. Treat and address
it as a friend, a brother, a partner with you in
the enterprise of life; you will find it a wonderful source of aid, encouragement and practical help and efficient service.**

Health Control. The Solar Plexus may b<

called upon to aid you in either stimulating
the action of any physical organ which may
have fallen into a habit of inactivity (probably
because of ill-usage or lack of proper treatment on your part); or in restoring normal
and healthy functioning in any physical organ
which may have become affected from any
reason. At the beginning, the "instinctive
mind" of the Solar Plexus fights against dis-
eased conditions, or inactive functioning: but,
in many cases, finding that it is not receiving
the proper co-operation on the part of the
"thinking mind" of the individual, it then
"makes the best of it," and tries to do the best
it can in the matter, under the circumstances.
When it finds you ready and willing to co-
operate with it in the matter of perfect or
ganic functioning, and improved physical condition, it will respond willingly and even
eagerly. **In such cases, however, it should
have its attention positively and clearly directed to the imperfectly functioning organ,
and to the nature of its shortcomings—together with an understanding of the undesirable effects to you arising from the same.**
In giving to the "instinctive mind" of the
Solar Plexus the proper information, instructions, and directions in the matter of restoring
physical health and proper functioning of the

organs, however, you should always bear in mind the fact that the Solar Plexus "understands its business"—**you do not have to tell it how to proceed** to secure the results from the organs in its care, for it understands this far better than can you. It has its own chemical laboratories; its machine-shops; its repair shops; and in fact a most wonderful establishment under its direction and care—and it knows how to run this, and it does run it right, providing that it is not hampered by conditions which it is unable to overcome.

Remember, always, that it, itself, represents **"the vis vita,"** the **"vis medicatrix naturæ,"** in short "Nature" itself within you, which cures diseases and strives to establish, maintain, and re-establish normal physical functioning. You do not need to tell it how to go about its work—that would be an impertinence. All that you need to do is to tell it that you are experiencing physical difficulties or weaknesses of such-and-such a nature or kind, and that such-and-such an organ does not seem to be functioning normally—in short that you are not obtaining normal results from certain organs or sets of organs. Impress this strongly upon the Solar Plexus, and let it know positively that it "is up to it" to get busy and remedy the trouble at its very

source. You are the officer on deck talking, as
to an equal, to the chief engineer below decks
in the engine room, the boiler room, and the
furnace rooms. Get this idea well fixed in your
mind, and you will know how to proceed correctly in the matter.

Furthermore, you must remember that you
have promised to do your part in the work
of establishing and maintaining the normal
physical conditions—you have promised your
full co-operation in the matter, and must live
up to this promise and agreement. If you
expect the Solar Plexus to do its share of the
work, you must be prepared to do yours. You
cannot expect to "lie down" on your end of the
job, and to have the Solar Plexus "keep busy"
on its end. If it finds you falling short, it will
be apt to do the same. You must "play fair"
with your partner in your work of Health and
Strength. You must see that the Solar Plexus
is not burdened with the work of taking care
of food of a wrong character, indigestible
masses, too much in quantity, and improperly
combined.

You must see that the body gets sufficient
exercise, sufficient rest, sufficient fresh air,
sufficient water, sufficient food of the right
kind, and that it is kept sufficiently cleaned. If
you insist upon sending down to it the mass

of indigestible stuff so commonly employed
as food, greasy, over-sweet, soggy, ill-cooked
stuff—you must not be surprised if the Solar
Plexus retaliates by first "firing it back" to
you; and then, if you persist, of "going on a
protest strike" and rendering you inefficient
service. You must "play fair" with the Solar
Plexus. It is good-natured, but is no fool; and
it has a high sense of justice and co-operation,
and resents any attempt to "put anything
over" on it, as many have found to their sor-
row and pain. Get on good terms with your
Solar Plexus—and play fair with it, if you are
wise.

Vital Force and Physical Energy. The Solar
Plexus is the source of Vital Force and Physical Energy—the great storehouse thereof,
as well as its generator. You may call upon it
for an increased supply thereof, and when it
becomes convinced of the actual necessity
therefor, it will respond. What is "Vital
Force" and "Physical Energy"? You know
very well what it is like when you feel it manifesting within yourself, and expressing itself
in your actions. You know very well what it
is like when you see it manifested by another
individual, and being expressed in his actions.
But find it hard to define it, or to explain it in
intelligent words.

You may think of it here as "the Steam of
Life"—the Power which causes the physical
machinery to move and the wheels go 'round.
It is what we mean when we say "vim,"
"vigor," "virility," "pep," "snap," and the like.
It is Nature's great vitalizing force, power,
and energy, which when manifested in physical action we call "Life." Or, again, we may
call it "Spirit," in the sense of "energy,"
"vivacity," "ardor," "enthusiasm," "courage,"
"animation," "vigor," etc.,—that which when
possesses it causes him to be termed "spir-
ited," and which when he lacks it causes him
to be termed "spiritless." Huxley says: "We
use the terms 'vitality,' and 'vital force' to denote great groups of natural operations, just
as we employ the names of 'electricity' or
'electrical force' to denote others." At the
last, Vital Force and Physical Energy must
be thought of as "Active Life-Power."

The Solar Plexus, through its "instinctive
mind" may be called upon by you for an
abundant supply of Vital Force or Physical
Energy—and it will respond quite as well as
in the cases previously mentioned. Tell it what
you want, and why you want it—and it will
begin to "get busy" to supply you with it. Co-
operate with it by maintaining the vigorous,
vital mental attitude—by seeing and thinking

of yourself as filled with Vital Force—by confidently expecting the flow thereof into your nervous system from the Solar Plexus, and, in short by being a "positive pole," instead of a "negative pole" in the scale of mental life.

Psychic Force. There is another phase of power inherent in the Solar Plexus, which we shall merely mention here, for it concerns a subject apart from that which constitutes the purpose of this book—yet we would fall short of that purpose were we to omit all reference to this additional power. This additional phase of power is that which, for want of a better name, may be called "Psychic Power." By "Psychic Power" is meant that peculiar force, power, or energy which when manifested by human beings is called "Odic Force," "Human Magnetism," "Vril," "Prana," "Ga-Lama," etc. It is the force which underlies the manifestations known as "Personal Magnetism," "Thought Force," "Mind Power," "Telepathy," "Thought Transference," etc., etc.,—in fact, all forms of manifestations in which the Directive Thought of man seems to take upon itself a physical form, and to act with a fine physical energy, when it flows from one mind or brain to others. Its vibrations constitute the "body" of the "mental currents," "thought waves," etc., while other of its quali-

ties constitute the energy thereof; the Direc
tive Thought involved in the "currents," etc.,
may be said to be the "soul" thereof.

While we do not care to go deeply into the
subject here, we feel free to say that this
Psychic Power may be obtained from the
Solar Plexus in precisely the same way in
which one obtains Vital Force or Physical
Energy from it—or as one causes it to act in
the direction of the control of the emotional
feelings, or in the restoration and preservation of physical health and normal functioning
of the physical organs. The general principle
of Awakening the Solar Plexus, and of then
inducing it to send forth its latent and inherent powers, forces, and energies in the direc-
iton indicated by you, is the same in all of the
cases. Understand the principle, and acquire
the "knack" of setting t... subtle forces into
operation, and you have the whole principle
at your command.

You are herewith warned, however, that
the use of Psychic Power for improper and
base motives, i.e., for instance, of psychically
influencing others against their own interests
and welfare, in order to gain an unworthy ad-
vantage over them, will bring about its own
punishment; for by so doing you set into operation certain psychic forces, of a similar na-

ture, which will prove your undoing and which will show you that you have "sown a wind, and reaped a whirlwind." For legitimate purposes, however, the Psychic Forces may be employed quite as freely and safely as the Physical Forces. Both are made for Use— not for Abuse. An understanding of the nature, source and character of this Psychic Power as herein stated, will serve to make clear to you many heretofore puzzling instances and phases of Psychic Phenomena.

VII

Solar Plexus Breathing-Exercises

The following Breathing Exercises will be found useful by you in your work of arousing the forces of the Solar Plexus, and of applying the energies thereof. There is a peculiar relation between the process of breathing and those of the Solar Plexus. The nature of this relation is far too technical to discuss in detail in this book; and, furthermore, the knowledge of the physiological-psychological nature of the principle involved is not essentially necessary for the effective practical application thereof in simple exercises or methods of application. Learn how to apply the practical methods, and let the matter of the technical scientific principles rest until you have time to "go deeply" into such subjects. Here follow the practical, simple exercises referred to.

Abdominal Breathing Stimulation

The Solar Plexus may be stimulated by an occasional exercise along the line of Abdominal Breathing is performed as follows: Inhale the breath in the ordinary manner, but instead of allowing it to rest in the upper part of the lungs, you should use the breathing-muscles so as to gently press the air downward toward the abdomen, so as to flatten out the diapraghm, i.e., that strong, flat plate-shaped muscle which divides the chest and its contents from the abdomen and its contents from the abdomen and its contents. This form of breathing is commonly known as "stomach breathing," or "breathing from the stomach." In this form of breathing, the abdomen is pressed outward in front, and at the sides; and the lower part of the lungs are filled with the air, instead of the latter being allowed to merely remain in the upper part of the lungs. It is difficult to closely describe the movements of this form of breathing, but you will gradually acquire them by following this general idea, i.e., (1) Breathe deeply, and (2) at the same time "bear down" gently in the region of the pit of the stomach, thus distending the abdomen in front and at the sides.

Practice this form of breathing, occasionally, and not continuing the exercise over a few minutes. Never strain unduly, and never tire out yourself. Use moderation and good judgment. The physical exercise should be accompanied by Directive Thought, i.e., thought directed to the Solar Plexus with the idea of arousing, and stimulating its activity —in short, giving the Solar Plexus a "mental massage," as it were. You may accompany this by a little "talk" to the "instinctive mind" of the Solar Plexus—such talk being "always in order," and always tending to work well.

The Invigorating Breath

The following exercise, accompanied by Directive Thought applied to the Solar Plexus, has been employed with excellent results in the direction of invigrating the whole system in a certain indescribable manner which must be experienced in order to be appreciated. It produces a stimulating reaction and invigoration, akin to that one experiences after a cold plunge followed with a good rubbing-down with a coarse towel.

(1) Inhale a full breath, through the nostrils. (2) Pucker up the lips as if you were going to use them in blowing a cornet or other brass wind-instrument—do not distend the cheeks, however, as in the case of the use of the instrument. (3) Exhale the breath, through the puckered lips, with a strong "blowing" motion and action just as if you

were trying to get a good, strong, clear note of a horn. Repeat several times; but do not over-exert or strain yourself, nor tire out yourself.

The Stimulating Breath

The following exercise has also been found quite stimulating, and many have discovered that it has improved the richness of the sound of their voices, and has given a new "tone" to their speaking and singing voice. It should be accompanied by Directive Thought applied to the Solar Plexus, as before described.

(1) Inhale a full breath, through the nostrils. (2) Open the mouth wide. (3) Then exhale the breath, "puffing" the air out of the mouth in one great "puff," like a locomotive, putting some life and vigor into the movement, though not straining yourself. Repeat several times; but do not tire yourself, nor employ the exercise too violently.

The "Nerve Force" Breath

The following breathing exercise is highly recommended by those who have had many years' experience with it. It is reported to have a decided value in the direction of energizing and stimulating the important nerve-

centres. Some call it the "nerve-bracing
breath," because it "braces up" the person
practicing it. It should be accompanied by
the Directive Thought applied to the Solar
Plexus, previously mentioned.

(1) Inhale a full breath, through the nostrils. (2) Retain the breath during the re-
mainder of the exercise, until you are directed to exhale it. (3) Extend the arms directly in front of you. (4) Contract the
muscles of the arms, and clench the fists;
then draw the fists slowly back until they
strike the shoulders, keeping the muscles
tensed during the process. (5) Keeping the
muscles still tensed, push the fists outward,
and then draw them backward, several times,
rather rapidly. (6) Exhale vigorously
through the mouth. Repeat several times,
avoiding over-exertion strain, or fatigue. The
exercise should be performed with "snap"
and energy.

The Quieting Breath

The following breathing exercise is highly
praised by those who have had long experience with it. It is said to quiet the nerves
when they have been under a strain, to re-
duce to normal the heart's action; to produce
a feeling of calm, tranquility, and restfulness.

It should be accompanied by the Directive Breath applied to the Solar Plexus, previously mentioned.

(1) Inhale a full breath, through the nostrils. (2) Bend slightly forward and exhale vigorously through the front part of your closed teeth—this, if properly performed, will produce a "hissing sound" like escaping steam. (3) Then, inhale once more through the nostrils. (4) Exhale vigorously, through the opened mouth, at the same time sounding (as if whispering) the word **"Hah!"** Conclude with ordinary, natural breaths, inhaled and exhaled in the ordinary manner. The exercise may then be repeated, varying the **"Hah"** exhalation by each time, successively, sounding one of the following words (as if whispering) in the same way, viz., **"Hee!" "Ho!" "Har!" "How!" "Hoo!" "Far!" "Fear!" "Four!"** Do not tire yourself, however, and stop whenever you feel like it, regardless of whether or not you have run through the whole list of whispered sounds.

The Grand Psychic Breath

The following breathing exercise, very popular in Oriental countries in which much attention is given to breathing methods, is known as "The Grand Psychic Breath," "The

Great Yogi Breath," or some similar name. The details of the exercise is variously stated by different Oriental writers, but the following form includes all of the important elements and movements, and is less technical than some other forms. In this exercise, the various parts of the body, as you will see as you proceed. It has been stated as "a general cleansing of the nervous system."

(1) Lie at ease, in a relaxed position. (2) Breathe tranquilly, easily, and rhythmically for a few moments, until the breath rhythm is secured and becomes regular. (3) Then, inhaling and exhaling, create the thought of the breath-current being drawn in, and then exhaled out from **each of the following parts of the body, in turn,** and in the following order: (a) the bones of the legs; (b) the bones of the arms; (c) the top of the skull; (d) the stomach; (e) the reproductive organism; (f) as travelling up and down the spinal column; (g) as inhaled and then exhaled through every pore in the skin. (4) Then, breathing rhythmically, by means of Directive Thought, send the current of Vital Force, and Phychic Force (combined) to the following great nervous centres of the body: (a) the forehead, (b) the back of the head, (c) the base of the brain, (d) the pit of the

stomach, (e) the lower part of the spine, (f) the region of the navel, and (g) the reproductive region. (5) Conclude by sweeping the entire body with currents of the combined Force, directed by Directive Thought. (6) Then rest a few minutes, breathing quietly, calmly and rhythmically, and enjoying the delightful feeling of rest, content, relaxation, and peacefulness which has come to you. Then rise, and go about your affairs, feeling like a "new man" or "new woman," by reason of the new and fresh strength that is in you.

Much in Little

In this book we have given you the essence, substance, gist, and spirit of the best teachings concerning the Solar Plexus, or Abdominal Brain,—teachings both Oriental and Occidental, both ancient and modern. The instruction has been condensed and compressed into a small space, and, therefore must be most carefully read and studied in order to obtain the full contents thereof. We ask you to read and re-read this book a number of times; taking it up from time to time to refresh your memory concerning its teachings. The subject is an important one, and the methods and instruction given you herein are practical and easily applied. Here you have

the gist of the Solar Plexus Teaching stated
in condensed form, without fanciful trim-
ming, fringes, or additions attached in order
to make the teachings "fit in" with some particular metaphysical theory. You have here
the essence—if you wish the rest, you may
add it for yourself quite as well, if not better,
than it has been added by certain writers and
teachers on the subject in the interest of their
own particular propaganda work.

COSIMO

COSIMO is a specialty publisher of books and publications that inspire, inform and engage readers. Our mission is to offer unique books to niche audiences around the world.

COSIMO CLASSICS offers a collection of distinctive titles by the great authors and thinkers throughout the ages. At COSIMO CLASSICS timeless classics find a new life as affordable books, covering a variety of subjects including: *Biographies, Business, History, Mythology, Personal Development, Philosophy, Religion and Spirituality,* and much more!

COSIMO-on-DEMAND publishes books and publications for innovative authors, non-profit organizations and businesses. COSIMO-on-DEMAND specializes in bringing books back into print, publishing new books quickly and effectively, and making these publications available to readers around the world.

COSIMO REPORTS publishes public reports that affect your world: from global trends to the economy, and from health to geo-politics.

9 7781